MRS BEETON'S
HOME COOKING

VEGETABLE DISHES

WARD LOCK LIMITED · LONDON

© Ward Lock Limited 1986

First published in Great Britain
in 1986 by Ward Lock Limited,
8 Clifford Street,
London W1X 1RB,
an Egmont Company.

Edited by Susan Dixon
Designed by Melissa Orrom
Text filmset in Caslon 540
by Cheney & Sons Limited
Printed and bound in Italy by
L.E.G.O.

**British Library Cataloguing in
Publication Data**

Vegetables.—
(Mrs. Beeton's home cooking)
  1. Cookery (Vegetables)
  I. Series
  641.6'5   TX801

ISBN 0-7063-6457-0

Notes
The recipes in this book have
been tested in metric weights
and measures. These have
been based on equivalents of
25g to 1 oz, 500g to 1 lb and
500ml to 1 pint, with some
adjustments where necessary.
  It is important to follow *either*
the metric *or* the imperial
measures. Do not use a
combination of measures.

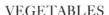

VEGETABLES

Persons in the flower of youth, having
healthy stomachs, and leading active
lives, may eat all sorts of vegetables,
without inconvenience, save, of course,
in excess. The digestive functions
possess great energy during the period of
youth: the body, to develop itself, needs
nourishment. Physical exercise gives an
appetite, which it is necessary to satisfy,
and vegetables cannot resist the vigorous
action of the gastric organs. But for aged
persons, the sedentary, or the delicate, it
is quite otherwise. Then the gastric
power has considerably diminished, the
digestive organs have lost their energy,
the process of digestion is consequently
slower, and the least excess at table is
followed by derangement of the stomach
for several days. Those who generally
digest vegetables with difficulty, should
eat them reduced to a pulp or purée, that
is to say, with their skins and tough fibres
removed. Subjected to this process,
vegetables which, when entire, would
create flatulence and wind, are then
comparatively harmless.

Isabella Beeton 1861

On pages 2 and 3
From the back, clockwise
Stuffed Tomatoes Provençale (page 52), *Breton Haricot Beans (page 9)*, and
Petits Pois à Française (page 37)

MRS BEETON'S ASPARAGUS PUDDING

3–4 helpings

150g/5oz asparagus heads
25g/1oz ham
2 × 15ml spoons/2 tablespoons
    flour
salt and pepper

4 eggs
25g/1oz softened butter
milk
fat for greasing

Chop the asparagus heads until they are the size of peas. Mince the ham very finely. Put into a bowl with the flour, asparagus, and seasoning. Beat the eggs well, and add with the butter to the asparagus with enough milk to make the mixture the consistency of a thick batter. Pour into a greased 500ml/1 pint mould or pudding basin. Cover securely with a double layer of buttered greaseproof paper or foil. Steam gently for 2 hours. Turn out on to a warmed serving dish and serve with melted butter poured round, but not over, the pudding.

BROAD BEANS WITH SPANISH SAUCE

4 helpings

1kg/2lb broad beans
1 small onion
375ml/¾ pint beef stock
2–3 sprigs thyme
1 bay leaf
100g/4oz button mushrooms

50g/2oz butter
25g/1oz flour
1 × 5ml spoon/1 teaspoon chopped
 parsley
1 × 5ml spoon/1 teaspoon lemon
 juice
salt and pepper

Shell the beans. Skin and chop the onion finely, and put into a saucepan with the stock, thyme, and bay leaf. Bring to the boil, add the beans, and cook for 15–20 minutes, or until tender. Drain and reserve the stock but discard the herbs.

Meanwhile, clean and slice the mushrooms. Melt the butter in a pan and fry the mushrooms; then remove from the pan with a perforated spoon, and add to the beans when cooked. Stir the flour into the remaining butter and cook for 1 minute, stirring all the time. Draw off the heat and gradually stir in the stock from the beans. Return to the heat and bring to the boil, stirring all the time. Add the beans and mushrooms, the parsley and the lemon juice, and season to taste.

BROAD BEAN.

BRETON HARICOT BEANS

4 helpings

200g/7oz haricot beans
1 clove of garlic
1 rasher streaky bacon
2 onions
2 cloves
a bunch of herbs (thyme, sage,
  savory, marjoram, parsley stalks)

salt and pepper
25g/1oz butter
1 × 15ml spoon/1 tablespoon
  concentrated tomato purée

GARNISH

1 × 15ml spoon/1 tablespoon
  chopped parsley

Cover the beans with cold water and leave to soak overnight. Skin and crush the garlic, and chop the bacon. Drain the beans, put into a saucepan, cover with fresh cold water and boil briskly for at least 10 minutes. Skin 1 onion, press the cloves into it, and add to the pan with the garlic, bacon, herbs, and seasoning. Cover and simmer for 1½ hours or until the beans are tender. Drain the beans, reserving 250ml/½ pint of the liquid, and discard the herbs, bacon, and onion. Skin and chop the remaining onion finely. Melt the butter in a pan and fry the onion gently for about 5 minutes. Add the tomato purée and the reserved bean stock. Cover and simmer gently for 10 minutes. Add the drained beans and simmer for a further 10 minutes. Garnish with the chopped parsley before serving.

BOSTON ROAST

6 helpings

300g/10oz haricot beans
1 onion
1 × 15ml spoon/1 tablespoon oil
150g/5oz Cheddar cheese
2 × 15ml spoons/2 tablespoons
    meat *or* vegetable stock *or* water

1 egg
100g/4oz soft white breadcrumbs
salt and pepper
fat for greasing

Cover the beans with cold water and leave to soak overnight. Drain well, put into a saucepan, cover with fresh cold water and boil briskly for at least 10 minutes. Cover and simmer gently for 1½ hours or until the beans are tender. Drain and mash them finely. Skin and chop the onion. Heat the oil in a frying pan and fry the onion until golden-brown. Grate the cheese. Put all the ingredients into a bowl and mix well. Shape the mixture into a loaf, place in a greased baking tin, and cover with buttered greaseproof paper. Bake in a moderate oven, 180°C/350°F/Gas 4, for 45 minutes.

Serve with gravy and vegetables.

Boston Roast

BEANS WITH SOURED CREAM

———————— *3–4 helpings* ————————

400g/13oz runner beans
125ml/¼ pint soured cream
½ × 2.5ml spoon/¼ teaspoon
  grated nutmeg
1 × 2.5ml spoon/½ teaspoon
  caraway seeds

salt and pepper
50g/2oz butter
50g/2oz soft white breadcrumbs

Prepare the beans and boil or steam them until just tender. Drain thoroughly. Mix the soured cream with the nutmeg, caraway seeds, and seasoning. Add the beans and toss well together. Grease a 1 litre/2 pint ovenproof dish with some of the butter and toss the breadcrumbs in it. Sprinkle them on top of the beans. Bake in a moderate oven, 180°C/350°F/Gas 4, for 30 minutes or until the topping is crisp and golden.

POLISH BEETROOT

6 helpings

800g/1lb 10oz cooked beetroot
1 small onion
15g/½ oz butter *or* margarine
2 × 15ml spoons/2 tablespoons
 flour

150g/5oz natural yoghurt
2 × 15ml spoons/2 tablespoons
 finely grated horseradish
salt and pepper
sugar (optional)

GARNISH

1 × 15ml spoon/1 tablespoon
 chopped parsley

Peel and grate the beetroot and skin and finely chop or grate the onion. Melt the fat in a saucepan and fry the onion gently for about 5 minutes. Stir in the flour and cook gently for 1 minute, stirring all the time. Draw off the heat and gradually stir in the yoghurt. Return to the heat, and bring to the boil, stirring all the time, until the sauce thickens. Add the beetroot and horseradish and heat thoroughly. Season to taste, and add sugar to taste, if liked. Serve hot, garnished with the parsley.

BEETROOT.

BUTTERED CARROTS

500ml/1 pint water
1 chicken stock cube
a pinch of white sugar
3 small carrots
3 spring onions
1 slice of bread

butter
25g/1oz Cheddar cheese
1 × 10ml spoon/1 dessertspoon
 chopped parsley
1 × 10ml spoon/1 dessertspoon
 butter

Bring the water to the boil in a saucepan, crumble in the stock cube and sugar, then draw off the heat. Prepare the carrots, and cut them into slices 6mm/¼ inch thick. Trim the onions, chop the green parts finely and add to the carrots. Halve and add the bulbs. Return the stock to the heat, add the vegetables, and simmer for 10 minutes; then drain. (Reserve the stock for soup or a drink.) Toast the bread, and butter it. Slice the cheese, and place it on the toast. Pile the vegetables on top, sprinkle with the parsley, and dot with the butter. Serve at once.

GERMAN CARROTS

6 helpings

625g/1¼lb carrots
½ small onion
50g/2oz butter *or* margarine
500ml/1 pint stock
extra stock

25g/1oz flour
a good pinch of grated nutmeg
1 × 15ml spoon/1 tablespoon
  chopped parsley
salt and pepper

Prepare the carrots, and skin and chop the onion finely. Melt half the fat in a heavy-based pan. Add the carrots and onion and cook very gently for 10 minutes, shaking the pan frequently so that the vegetables do not stick to the bottom. Pour the stock over the carrots, cover the pan, and simmer gently for 10–15 minutes or until the carrots are tender. Drain the carrots, reserving the cooking liquor, and keep them warm. Make the cooking liquor up to 375ml/¾ pint with extra stock, if necessary. Melt the remaining fat in a saucepan. Add the flour and cook gently for 1 minute, stirring all the time. Draw off the heat and gradually stir in the stock. Return to the heat and bring to the boil, stirring all the time. Add the carrots, nutmeg and parsley, and season to taste. Serve as soon as possible.

CARROTS.

GLAZED CARROTS

6 helpings

625g/1¼lb young carrots
50g/2oz butter
3 sugar lumps

½ × 2.5ml spoon/¼ teaspoon salt
beef stock

GARNISH

1 × 15ml spoon/1 tablespoon
  chopped parsley

Prepare the carrots but leave them whole. Heat the butter in a saucepan. Add the carrots, sugar, salt, and enough stock to half cover the carrots. Cook gently, without a lid, for 15–20 minutes or until the carrots are tender, shaking the pan occasionally. Remove the carrots with a perforated spoon and keep warm. Boil the stock rapidly in the pan until it is reduced to a rich glaze. Replace the carrots, 2–3 at a time, and turn them in the glaze until they are thoroughly coated. Place on a serving dish and garnish with parsley before serving.

Overleaf
From the back, clockwise
Cauliflower Cheese (page 20), Glazed Carrots (above) and
Leeks in Parmesan Sauce (page 25)

CAULIFLOWER CHEESE

1 medium-sized firm cauliflower
2 × 15ml spoons/2 tablespoons
   butter *or* margarine
4 × 15ml spoons/4 tablespoons
   flour
200ml/8fl oz milk

125g/5oz grated Cheddar cheese
a pinch of dry mustard
a pinch of Cayenne pepper
salt and pepper
25g/1oz fine dry white
   breadcrumbs

Prepare the cauliflower. Put the head in a saucepan containing enough boiling salted water to half-cover it. Cover the pan, and cook gently for 20–30 minutes until tender. Drain well, reserving 175ml/7fl oz of the cooking water. Break the head carefully into sections, and place in a warmed ovenproof dish. Keep warm under greased greaseproof paper.

Melt the fat in a medium-sized pan, stir in the flour, and cook for 2–3 minutes, stirring all the time, without letting the flour colour. Mix together the milk and reserved cooking water, and gradually add to the pan, stirring all the time to prevent lumps forming. Bring the sauce to the boil, lower the heat, and simmer until thickened. Remove from the heat, and stir in 100g/4oz of the cheese, with the mustard and Cayenne pepper. Season to taste. Stir until the cheese is fully melted, then pour the sauce over the cauliflower. Mix the remaining cheese with the breadcrumbs, and sprinkle them on top. Place in a hot oven, 220°C/425°F/Gas 7, for 7–10 minutes, to brown the top. Serve at once.

Note A mixture of 2 × 15ml spoons/2 tablespoons grated Cheddar cheese and 1 × 15ml spoon/1 tablespoon grated Parmesan cheese can be used for sprinkling, if liked, or 1–2 crumbled, crisply fried rashers of streaky bacon.

CAULIFLOWER WITH RICH MUSHROOM SAUCE

4–6 helpings

1kg/2lb cauliflower (approx)
50g/2oz butter
25g/1oz flour
375ml/¾ pint chicken *or* vegetable
   stock *or* milk
100g/4oz button mushrooms
3 egg yolks

1 × 15ml spoon/1 tablespoon
   lemon juice
salt and black pepper
a pinch of grated nutmeg
4–6 slices bread
butter

Prepare the cauliflower. Break it into medium-sized florets and boil or steam them until just tender. Drain thoroughly and keep hot. Melt the 50g/2oz butter in a pan, stir in the flour, and cook for 1 minute. Draw off the heat and gradually stir in the stock or milk. Return to the heat and bring to the boil, stirring all the time, until the sauce thickens. Clean and chop the mushrooms finely, add to the sauce, and simmer gently for 5 minutes. Beat the egg yolks lightly, beat in the lemon juice and 2 × 15ml spoons/2 tablespoons of the hot sauce, then stir into the sauce. Heat gently, but do not allow the sauce to boil after the egg yolks have been added or it will curdle. Season to taste and add the nutmeg.

Toast the bread, cut into rounds, and butter each. Arrange the cauliflower neatly on the rounds, and pour the sauce over. Serve as soon as possible.

POLISH CAULIFLOWER

4 helpings

1 large cauliflower	2 hard-boiled eggs
50g/2oz butter *or* margarine	1 × 15ml spoon/1 tablespoon
50g/2oz soft white breadcrumbs	chopped parsley

Prepare and cook the cauliflower until just tender. Meanwhile, heat the fat in a frying pan and fry the breadcrumbs until they are crisp and golden. Chop the egg whites finely and sieve the yolks. Drain the cauliflower thoroughly and place on a serving dish. Sprinkle the breadcrumbs and then the egg yolk and parsley over the cauliflower. Arrange the chopped egg white round the edge of the dish.

Polish Cauliflower

STUFFED COURGETTES

4 helpings

1 × 10ml spoon/1 dessertspoon salt
1 litre/2 pints water
1kg/2lb courgettes

25g/1oz butter for greasing
100g/4oz grated Parmesan cheese
chopped herbs

STUFFING

50g/2oz onion
1 clove of garlic
150g/5oz mushrooms
50ml/2fl oz cooking oil
150g/5oz lean ham

50g/2oz soft white breadcrumbs
1 egg
salt
a pinch of ground mace
black pepper

Add the salt to the water in a saucepan and bring it to the boil. Add the courgettes and cook for 8 minutes. Drain and cut in half lengthways. Scoop out the pulp and put it into a small bowl. Keep the skins aside.

To make the stuffing, prepare and chop the onion, garlic, and mushrooms. Heat the oil and sauté the vegetables for 5 minutes. Remove from the heat and keep aside. Mince the ham finely and mix with the breadcrumbs and courgette pulp. Add to the pan, return to the heat and cook for 3 minutes. Turn the mixture into a large bowl. Beat the egg until liquid and season well with salt, mace, and pepper; then add enough egg to the main mixture to make a paste soft enough to be spooned. Season generously.

Fill the courgette skins with the mixture and level the surfaces. Place on a baking tray well greased with soft butter. Sprinkle the stuffed courgettes with the cheese and bake in a moderate oven, 180°C/350°F/Gas 4, for 15–20 minutes until the cheese is melted and golden-brown. Brush once or twice with butter while baking. Sprinkle with chopped herbs, and serve hot.

LEEKS IN PARMESAN SAUCE

— *4 helpings* —

1kg/2lb leeks
1 litre/2 pints water
1 × 10ml spoon/1 dessertspoon salt
25g/1oz butter *or* margarine
25g/1oz plain flour
300ml/12fl oz well-flavoured
    vegetable stock

150ml/6fl oz single cream
salt and pepper
a pinch of grated nutmeg
1 chicken stock cube
50g/2oz grated Parmesan cheese

GARNISH

1 × 15ml spoon/1 tablespoon
    chopped parsley and chives,
    mixed

Prepare the leeks and keep them whole; tie up in a bundle. Bring the water and salt to the boil in a saucepan and cook the leeks for 20 minutes, then drain well. Put to one side.

Meanwhile, melt the fat in a samll pan, add the flour, and cook for about 4 minutes, stirring until the mixture looks like wet sand. Add the stock gradually, stirring all the time, to make a sauce. Bring to the boil, lower the heat, and stir until the mixture thickens. Stir in the cream, a little salt and simmer gently for 5 minutes. Crumble the stock cube into the sauce. Boil for 5 minutes longer. Remove from the heat, and scatter in half the grated cheese. Untie the bundle of leeks. Put in a long, shallow, flameproof dish and cover with the sauce. Sprinkle with the remaining cheese, and brown under the grill for 5–6 minutes. Sprinkle the herbs on top just before serving.

SPICED LENTILS

500g/1lb red lentils
1 litre/2 pints water
1 × 2.5ml spoon/½ teaspoon sea
  salt *or* 1 × 5ml spoon/1 teaspoon
  table salt
1 onion
1 × 5ml spoon/1 teaspoon turmeric
1 × 5ml spoon/1 teaspoon crushed
  root *or* ground ginger

3 tomatoes
2 whole cardamoms
3 × 15ml spoons/3 tablespoons
  cooking oil
1 × 5ml spoon/1 teaspoon crushed
  garlic
1 × 5ml spoon/1 teaspoon ground
  coriander
a pinch of chilli powder

GARNISH

chopped fresh coriander leaves

finely chopped *or* grated onion

Put the lentils into a large pan and cover with the water and salt. Bring to the boil, reduce the heat, and simmer for 30–45 minutes until tender. Drain and put to one side.

Meanwhile, skin and chop the onion, and mix with the turmeric and ginger. Chop the tomatoes, and crush the cardamoms in a pestle and mortar, or grind in a coffee or nut mill. Heat the oil in a large deep frying pan, add the onion, ginger and turmeric, and fry gently until soft and lightly browned. Add the tomatoes and all the remaining ingredients, and fry for 3–4 minutes, stirring all the time. Remove from the heat.

Add the lentils to the mixture in the pan, and mix thoroughly to coat them with oil. Replace over moderate heat, and cook until well heated through and quite mushy. Serve very hot, sprinkled with the coriander leaves and onion.

Note Although hot and spicy, this dish is not as hot as a curry. It can be served as an accompaniment to any pasta, pulse or plainly cooked root vegetable dish, or with a green vegetable salad as a main course dish.

Spiced Lentils

LETTUCE WITH HERB SAUCE

6 helpings

6 small lettuces
salt
25g/1oz butter *or* margarine
25g/1oz flour
250ml/½ pint chicken *or* vegetable
  stock

1 × 10ml spoon/1 dessertspoon
  chopped chives
1 bay leaf
1 × 10ml spoon/1 dessertspoon
  chopped parsley
pepper

Trim and wash the lettuces. Plunge into boiling salted water for 2 minutes and then drain. Refresh in cold water and drain thoroughly. Melt the fat in a saucepan. Stir in the flour and cook for 1 minute without browning, stirring all the time. Draw off the heat and gradually stir in the stock. Return to the heat and bring to the boil, stirring all the time, until the sauce thickens. Add the herbs and seasoning and then add the lettuces. Cover and cook gently for 30 minutes, stirring from time to time. Remove the bay leaf. Re-season if required before serving.

MUSHROOMS WITH CHEESE

400g/13oz flat mushrooms
butter *or* margarine for greasing
salt and pepper
1 × 15ml spoon/1 tablespoon
  chopped chives
1 × 15ml spoon/1 tablespoon
  chopped parsley

1 × 15ml spoon/1 tablespoon soft
  white breadcrumbs
2 × 15ml spoons/2 tablespoons
  grated Parmesan cheese
25g/1oz butter

Clean the mushrooms and remove the stalks. These can be cooked with the caps or kept and used as a flavouring in another dish. Place the mushrooms, gills uppermost, in a greased ovenproof dish and season. Sprinkle with the chives and parsley. Mix the breadcrumbs and cheese together and sprinkle them over the mushrooms. Melt the butter and sprinkle it over the top. Bake, uncovered, in a fairly hot oven, 190°C/375°F/Gas 5, for 25 minutes.

MUSHROOMS.

STUFFED MUSHROOMS

6 helpings

12 large flat mushrooms
fat for greasing
1 medium-sized onion
25g/1oz butter *or* margarine
50g/2oz cooked ham
1 × 15ml spoon/1 tablespoon soft
white breadcrumbs

1 × 10ml spoon/1 dessertspoon
grated Parmesan cheese
1 × 10ml spoon/1 dessertspoon
chopped parsley
white wine
salt and pepper

Clean the mushrooms and remove the stalks. Place the caps in a well-greased ovenproof dish, gills uppermost, and chop the stalks finely. Skin and chop the onion finely. Melt the fat in a pan and fry the mushroom stalks and onion gently for 5 minutes. Chop the ham finely and add to the onion mixture together with the breadcrumbs, cheese, and parsley. Add enough white wine just to bind the mixture together, and season well. Divide the stuffing mixture between the mushroom caps. Cover and bake in a fairly hot oven, 190°C/375°F/Gas 5, for 25 minutes.

Note If liked, the mushrooms can be served on croûtes of toast or fried bread.

Stuffed Mushrooms

ONIONS AND APPLES

4 helpings

300g/10oz onions
400g/13oz cooking apples
3 × 15ml spoons/3 tablespoons
   butter *or* margarine

1 × 10ml spoon/1 dessertspoon
   sugar
salt and pepper

Skin and blanch the onions. Drain and cut them into rings. Peel, core, and slice the apples. Melt the fat in a pan and add the onions, apples and sugar. Cover and simmer gently for about 30 minutes or until tender. Season to taste and serve.

ONIONS IN CIDER WITH TOMATOES

6 helpings

6 large onions
200g/7oz tomatoes
50g/2oz butter *or* margarine
2 bay leaves
2 cloves

2 × 15ml spoons/2 tablespoons
   cider
250ml/½ pint vegetable stock
salt and pepper

Skin and blanch the onions. Drain and cut them into rings. Skin and slice the tomatoes. Melt the fat in a pan. Add the onion rings and fry gently until golden. Add the tomatoes, bay leaves, cloves, cider, and stock. Cover and simmer gently for 45 minutes. Season to taste and serve with the cooking liquor.

GLAZED ONIONS

400g/13oz button onions
chicken stock
salt and pepper
1 × 15ml spoon/1 tablespoon light
  soft brown sugar

25g/1oz butter
a pinch of grated nutmeg

Skin the onions and put them in a saucepan into which they just fit in one layer. Add just enough stock to cover them. Heat to simmering point, and simmer for 15–20 minutes until the onions are just tender, adding a very little extra hot stock if needed. When the onions are ready, the stock should be reduced almost to a glaze. Remove from the heat, and add the rest of the ingredients. Turn the onions over with a spoon to blend the extra seasonings well with the stock and to coat the onions. Return to the heat, and shake the onions in the pan, until the glaze and fat give them a shiny brown coating. Serve at once, with the remaining syrupy glaze.

Note Glazed onions are often used as a garnish.

ONION.

SCALLOPED OKRA AND TOMATOES

300g/10oz okra
milk
200g/7oz tomatoes
salt and pepper
3 × 15ml spoons/3 tablespoons
  butter *or* margarine

25g/1oz flour
2 × 15ml spoons/2 tablespoons soft
  white breadcrumbs

Wash the okra and cook in boiling salted water for 15 minutes. Drain, reserving the cooking liquor. Make the liquor up to 250ml/½ pint with milk, if necessary. Cut the okra into small pieces and slice the tomatoes. Divide the okra and tomatoes between 6 scallop shells or small ramekin dishes. Season with salt and pepper. Melt 2 × 15ml spoons/2 tablespoons of the fat in a pan. Stir in the flour and cook for 1 minute without browning, stirring all the time. Draw off the heat and gradually stir in the cooking liquor and milk. Return to the heat and bring to the boil, stirring all the time, until the sauce thickens. Re-season if required. Pour this over the okra and tomatoes. Sprinkle with the breadcrumbs and dot with the remaining fat. Bake in a fairly hot oven, 190°C/375°F/Gas 5, for 15–20 minutes. Serve hot in the scallop shells or ramekin dishes.

Scalloped Okra and Tomatoes

PARSNIP AND APPLE CASSEROLE

---
6 helpings

400g/13oz parsnips
200ml/8fl oz apple sauce
fat for greasing
75g/3oz brown sugar
salt
1 × 2.5ml spoon/½ teaspoon
  grated nutmeg

1 × 15ml spoon/1 tablespoon
  lemon juice
75g/3oz butter
75g/3oz soft white breadcrumbs
½ × 2.5ml spoon/¼ teaspoon
  paprika

Prepare and boil or steam the parsnips. Mash or sieve them. Arrange with the apple sauce in layers in a greased casserole. Sprinkle each layer with brown sugar, salt, nutmeg, lemon juice, and flakes of butter. Top with the breadcrumbs and sprinkle with paprika. Cook in a fairly hot oven, 190°C/375°F/Gas 5, for 30 minutes.

PETITS POIS À LA FRANÇAISE

6 helpings

1 lettuce heart
1 bunch spring onions
50g/2oz butter
750g/1½ lb fresh shelled *or* frozen
  peas

salt and pepper
a pinch of sugar

Shred the lettuce and chop the spring onions. Melt the butter in a pan, add the lettuce, spring onions, peas, seasoning, and sugar. Cover and simmer gently for 10–15 minutes or until the peas are very tender. Re-season if required before serving.

Note Frozen peas may take even less than 10 minutes; well-grown fresh garden peas may take 20–25 minutes.

GREEN PEA.

PEASE PUDDING

625g/1¼lb split peas
1 small onion
bouquet garni

salt and pepper
50g/2oz butter *or* margarine
2 eggs

Soak the peas overnight. Drain, put into a pan, and cover with fresh cold water. Skin the onion and add to the pan with the bouquet garni and seasoning. Cover and simmer the peas slowly for about 2–2½ hours or until they are tender. Drain thoroughly and sieve or process in an electric blender. Cut the fat into small pieces, beat the eggs until liquid, and add both to the pea purée with the seasoning. Beat well together. Place the mixture in a floured cloth and tie tightly. Simmer gently in boiling salted water for 1 hour. Remove from the pan, take out of the cloth, and serve very hot.

Serve with sausages or pickled pork.

Pease Pudding

PEPPERS WITH APPLE

3–4 helpings

1 large cooking apple
100g/4oz Gruyère cheese
3–4 large green peppers
1 small green pepper
25g/1oz butter *or* margarine

25g/1oz flour
250ml/½ pint milk
salt and freshly ground black
  pepper
butter *or* margarine for greasing

GARNISH (OPTIONAL)

1 thickly sliced tomato

3–4 button mushroom caps

Peel, core, and chop the apple into small pieces. Grate the cheese. Wash the large peppers and cut off the tops. Discard the membranes and the seeds, but keep the caps. Blanch the peppers and their caps. Drain. Chop the small pepper finely. Melt the fat, stir in the flour, and cook together over gentle heat for 2–3 minutes, stirring all the time. Do not let the flour colour. Draw off the heat and gradually stir in the milk, without letting lumps form. Return to the heat, bring to the boil, and simmer until very thick, stirring occasionally. Season to taste. Mix in the chopped apple, grated cheese, and chopped pepper. Trim the bases of the other peppers so that they stand steadily, cut sides uppermost. Spoon the stuffing mixture into the peppers and replace the caps. Place the peppers, cut side uppermost on a lightly greased baking tray. Bake in a cool oven, 150°C/300°F/Gas 2, for 25–30 minutes. Garnish, if liked, with the sliced tomato and mushroom caps before serving.

POTATOES BYRON

1kg/2lb potatoes
salt and pepper
a good pinch of grated nutmeg
100g/4oz butter

flour
125ml/¼ pint single cream
50g/2oz grated Parmesan cheese

Wash and bake the potatoes in their skins in a fairly hot oven, 190–200°C/375–400°F/Gas 5–6, for 1–1½ hours. When cooked, cut them in half and scoop the pulp into a basin. Season with salt, pepper, and nutmeg. Add 75g/3oz of the butter and beat the mixture well with a wooden spoon. Divide into 6 or 8 portions and mould into medallion shapes, 1.25–2.5cm/½–1 inch thick, on a floured surface. Heat the remaining butter in a frying pan and fry the potatoes gently on both sides until golden-brown. Remove from the pan and put in an ovenproof dish. Either spoon the cream over each potato medallion and sprinkle with the cheese, or add half the cheese to the white sauce, spoon it over the potatoes, then sprinkle with the remaining cheese. Place the dish under a moderate grill until the cheese is golden-brown.

TORTILLA ESPAGNOLA
(Spanish Omelet)

4 helpings

750g/1½lb potatoes
250g/8oz onions
olive oil for shallow frying

salt
6 eggs

Peel and dice the potatoes. Skin and slice the onions, and mix them together. Put enough oil into a large frying pan to cover the bottom by 6mm/¼ inch. Heat the oil until very hot, then add the potatoes and onions, and sprinkle with salt. Fry gently for about 20 minutes until soft but not crisp. Turn over or stir gently from time to time. Remove the vegetables from the pan with a perforated spoon.

Beat the eggs lightly with a pinch of salt, and stir into the fried vegetable mixture. Drain off any oil, clean the pan, and heat 1 × 5ml spoon/1 teaspoon oil in it until very hot. Pour in the egg and vegetable mixture, and cook briefly, shaking the pan vigorously to prevent the mixture sticking. Slide the half-cooked omelet on to a large plate, turn it over on to a second plate, then slide it back into the pan, uncooked side down. Cook for another 2–3 minutes to brown the second side, shaking as before.

The finished tortilla should be about 2.5cm/1 inch thick, crisp on the outside, and juicy in the middle.

Serve with a green salad.

Tortilla Espagnola

DUCHESSE POTATOES

Makes 500g/1lb (approx)

500g/1lb old potatoes
25g/1oz butter *or* margarine
1 egg *or* 2 egg yolks
salt and pepper

a little grated nutmeg (optional)
butter *or* margarine for greasing
a little beaten egg for brushing

Prepare the potatoes, and boil or steam them. Drain thoroughly, and sieve. Beat in the fat and egg or egg yolks. Season to taste with salt and pepper and add the nutmeg, if used. Spoon the mixture into a piping bag fitted with a large rose nozzle and pipe rounds of potato on to a greased baking tray. Brush with a little beaten egg. Bake in a fairly hot oven, 200°C/400°F/Gas 6, for about 15 minutes or until the potatoes are a good golden-brown.

Note The potatoes can be piped on to the baking tray and then baked when required. If a piping bag is not available, shape the potato into diamonds, rounds or triangles. Criss-cross the tops with a knife, brush with the egg, and bake as above.

POTATOES PARISIENNE

—— 4–6 helpings ——

1kg/2lb potatoes
25g/1oz butter
1 × 15ml spoon/1 tablespoon oil
½ × 2.5ml spoon/¼ teaspoon salt
3 × 15ml spoons/3 tablespoons
    softened butter

3 × 15ml spoons/3 tablespoons
    chopped fresh mixed herbs
    (parsley, chives, tarragon)
pepper

Peel the potatoes and cut into small, round balls, using a potato ball scoop. Dry in a clean cloth. Heat the butter and oil in a frying pan large enough to hold all the potatoes in 1 layer. Put in the potatoes and coat evenly in the fat. Fry them gently until the potatoes are a light golden colour all over. Reduce the heat, sprinkle with the salt and cover the pan. Continue frying very gently for 12–15 minutes, shaking the pan frequently, until the potatoes are tender. Drain off the fat. Raise the heat and shake the potatoes in the pan until sizzling. Remove from the heat, add the softened butter and herbs, season well with pepper, and roll the potatoes round the pan until coated with herbs. Arrange round a meat dish or serve separately in a warmed dish.

Note Carrots, turnips, and similar vegetables can be cooked in the same way as the potatoes.

Overleaf
From the left
Potatoes Lyonnaise (page 48), *Potatoes Byron (page 41)* and
Potatoes Parisienne (above)

POTATOES LYONNAISE

6 helpings

1kg/2lb potatoes
250g/8oz onions
75g/3oz butter *or* margarine

salt and pepper
1 × 15ml spoon/1 tablespoon
chopped parsley

Scrub the potatoes, but do not peel them. Boil or steam them in their skins until tender. Drain, peel, and cut into slices 6mm /¼ inch thick. Skin and slice the onions thinly. Melt the fat in a frying pan and fry the onions gently until they are just golden. Remove from the pan, put on one side, and keep warm. Add the potatoes to the pan and fry on both sides until crisp and golden. Replace the onions in the pan and mix with the potatoes. Season to taste with salt and pepper, turn into a serving dish, and sprinkle with the parsley.

POTATOES.

POTATO CROQUETTES

Makes 12–15

500g/1lb old potatoes
25g/1oz butter *or* margarine
1 egg *or* 2 egg yolks
salt and pepper
1 × 5ml spoon/1 teaspoon chopped parsley *or* 2 × 15ml spoons/2 tablespoons grated Parmesan *or* Cheddar cheese (optional)

2 eggs
flour for dusting
dried white breadcrumbs for coating
fat *or* oil for deep frying

Prepare the potatoes and boil or steam them. Drain thoroughly, and sieve. Beat in the fat and egg or egg yolks, and season to taste. Add the parsley or grated cheese, if used. Beat the eggs until liquid, form the potato into balls or cylindrical rolls, dust with flour, and coat twice with egg and breadcrumbs. If possible, chill for 1 hour before frying. Heat the fat or oil to 190°C/375°F, and fry the potato croquettes or balls until golden-brown. Drain thoroughly and serve as soon as possible.

ITALIAN SPINACH

---
4 helpings

25g/1oz butter *or* margarine
1kg/2lb spinach
salt and pepper
25g/1oz sultanas

1 clove of garlic
2 × 15ml spoons/2 tablespoons
 olive oil
25g/1oz pine kernels

Melt the butter in a pan, add the wet spinach leaves, season with salt, then cover and cook slowly for about 10 minutes or until the spinach is tender. Drain thoroughly; then chop coarsely. Cover the sultanas with boiling water for 1 minute to plump them; then drain thoroughly. Skin and crush the garlic. Heat the oil in a wide pan. Add the spinach, garlic, and seasoning. Turn the spinach over and over in the pan to heat it thoroughly without frying. Add the sultanas and nuts and serve hot.

CORN PUDDING

---
6 helpings

100g/4oz plain flour
1 × 5ml spoon/1 teaspoon salt
1 × 2.5ml spoon/½ teaspoon black
 pepper
2 eggs

500ml/1 pint milk
400g/13oz fresh *or* frozen
 sweetcorn kernels
fat for greasing

Sift the flour, salt, and pepper. Beat the eggs until liquid and add them to the flour, stirring well. Beat together with the milk and then the corn to form a batter. Turn into a greased 1.5 litre/3 pint pie or ovenproof dish and bake in a moderate oven, 180°C/350°F/Gas 4, for 1 hour. Serve hot.

Italian Spinach and *Corn Pudding*

STUFFED TOMATOES PROVENÇALE

4 helpings

8 medium-sized tomatoes
salt and pepper
50g/2oz onions *or* shallots
1 small clove of garlic
1 × 15ml spoon/1 tablespoon olive
  oil

25g/1oz butter
75–100g/3–4oz soft white
  breadcrumbs
1 × 15ml spoon/1 tablespoon
  chopped parsley

Halve the tomatoes crossways. Remove the pips and juice and place the tomatoes in an ovenproof dish. Season lightly with salt and pepper. Skin and chop the onion or shallots finely. Skin and crush the garlic. Heat the oil in a pan and fry the onion and garlic gently without browning. Add the butter and heat until melted; then add the breadcrumbs and parsley. Season to taste and mix well together. Spoon this mixture into the tomato halves. Bake in a hot oven, 220°C/425°F/Gas 7, for 15 minutes or until the breadcrumbs are lightly browned.

TOMATO AND ONION PIE

4 helpings

400g/13oz onions, preferably
  Spanish
50g/2oz butter
800g/1lb 10oz tomatoes

50g/2oz Cheddar cheese
fat for greasing
salt and pepper
50g/2oz soft white breadcrumbs

Skin the onions, put into a bowl, and cover with boiling water. Leave for 5 minutes, drain, dry thoroughly, and cut into slices. Melt half the butter in a pan and fry the onions until golden-brown. Skin and slice the tomatoes, and grate the cheese. Place the onions and tomatoes in alternate layers in a greased pie dish, sprinkle each layer lightly with salt and pepper and liberally with cheese and some of the breadcrumbs. Cover the whole with a layer of breadcrumbs and dot with the remaining butter. Bake in a fairly hot oven, 190°C/375°F/Gas 5, for 45 minutes.

THE TOMATO.

MARROW WITH TOMATOES

400g/13oz tomatoes	1 medium-sized marrow
25g/1oz butter *or* margarine	salt and pepper

GARNISH

1 × 10ml spoon/1 dessertspoon chopped parsley	1 × 10ml spoon/1 dessertspoon chopped chives

Skin the tomatoes and cut into slices. Melt the fat in a saucepan. Add the tomatoes and cook gently for 10 minutes. Peel the marrow, discard the seeds, and cut the flesh into 2.5cm/1 inch squares. Add to the tomatoes and season with salt and pepper. Cover the pan with a tight-fitting lid and cook the marrow gently for 20 minutes or until tender. Re-season if required before serving. Garnish with the parsley and chives.

Marrow with Tomatoes

VEGETABLE AND NUT FRICASSÉE

3–4 helpings

1 medium-sized onion	75g/3oz cashew nuts *or* pine
2 sticks celery	kernels
25g/1oz margarine	salt and pepper
50g/2oz flour	2–3 × 15ml spoons/2–3
500ml/1 pint milk	tablespoons single cream

GARNISH

cooked spinach *or* green peas	cooked carrots

Skin the onion, and chop finely with the celery. Melt the margarine in a pan and fry the onion and celery gently for a few minutes, without browning. Stir in the flour and cook for 1 minute. Draw off the heat and gradually stir in the milk. Return to the heat and bring to the boil, stirring all the time, until the sauce thickens. Add the nuts and seasoning. Cover the pan, reduce the heat, and simmer gently for 15 minutes. Stir in the cream and re-season if required.

Make a border of the spinach or peas on a hot dish. Pour the fricassée into the centre of the dish and garnish with the carrot, cut into matchsticks. Serve hot.

RATATOUILLE

4 helpings

250g/8oz onions (approx)
1 clove of garlic
100g/4oz green pepper (approx)
200g/7oz aubergine (approx)
200g/7oz courgettes
400g/13oz tomatoes

4 × 15ml spoons/4 tablespoons
  olive oil
sat and pepper
1 × 2.5ml spoon/½ teaspoon
  coriander seeds

GARNISH

1 × 15ml spoon/1 tablespoon
  chopped parsley

Skin the onions and slice in rings. Skin and crush the garlic.
Remove the membranes and seeds from the pepper and cut the
flesh into thin strips. Cut the unpeeled aubergine and courgettes
into 1.25cm/½ inch slices. Skin and chop the tomatoes roughly.

Heat 2 × 15ml spoons/2 tablespoons of the oil in a pan and
gently fry the onions, garlic, and pepper for about 10 minutes. Add
the remaining oil, the aubergine, and the courgettes. Cover and
simmer gently for 30 minutes, stirring occasionally to prevent the
vegetables from sticking to the bottom. Add the tomatoes,
seasoning and coriander seeds, and simmer for a further 15
minutes. Serve hot or cold, garnished with the parsley.

GARLIC.

PEPERONATA

4 helpings

300g/10oz tomatoes
1 large onion
1 large red pepper
2 large green peppers
1 large yellow pepper *or* 1 extra red
  pepper

3 × 15ml spoons/3 tablespoons
  olive oil
1 × 2.5ml spoon/½ teaspoon
  coriander seeds (optional)
salt and pepper

Skin the tomatoes, cut into quarters, and remove the seeds. Skin and slice the onion. Skin the peppers, remove the membranes and seeds, and chop the flesh. Heat the oil in a frying pan, add the onion, and fry for 5 minutes. Lightly crush the coriander seeds, if used. Add the tomatoes, peppers, coriander seeds, and seasoning to the pan. Cover and cook gently for 1 hour, stirring from time to time. Re-season if required before serving. Serve hot or cold.

Peperonata

VEGETABLE CASSEROLE

4–6 helpings

400g/13oz onions
2 cloves garlic
2 green peppers
400g/13oz courgettes
2 medium-sized aubergines
400g/13oz tomatoes
2 × 15ml spoons/2 tablespoons oil
200g/7oz mushrooms
75g/3oz concentrated tomato purée
2 bay leaves

1 × 15ml spoon/1 tablespoon
  chopped parsley
1 × 5ml spoon/1 teaspoon chopped
  marjoram
1 × 5ml spoon/1 teaspoon chopped
  thyme
salt and pepper
250ml/½ pint vegetable stock *or*
  water
400g/13oz potatoes
25g/1oz butter

Skin and chop the onions and skin and crush the garlic. Remove the membranes and seeds from the peppers and chop the flesh. Slice the unpeeled courgettes and aubergines and skin and slice the tomatoes. Heat the oil in a frying pan and fry the onions, garlic, and peppers for 5 minutes. Turn into a 3 litre/6 pint casserole with the courgettes, aubergines, tomatoes, mushrooms, tomato purée, herbs, and seasoning. Mix well and pour in the stock or water. Peel and slice the potatoes thinly, and arrange on the top. Dot with the butter, and cover. Bake in a moderate oven, 180°C/350°F/Gas 4, for 1 hour. Remove the lid and bake for a further 30 minutes or until the potatoes are golden-brown.

MIXED VEGETABLES

6 helpings

750g/1½lb mixed vegetables
  parsnips, turnips, carrots, leeks,
  cauliflower *or* broad beans, peas,
  spring onions, tomatoes, new
  carrots, new turnips

25g/1oz butter *or* margarine
100–150ml/4–6fl oz boiling water
salt and pepper

GARNISH

1 × 15ml spoon/1 tablespoon
  chopped parsley

Prepare the vegetables; then thinly slice the parsnips, turnips,
carrots, and leeks, if used, splitting the slices into halves or
quarters if large. Break the cauliflower into florets. Leave most of
the other vegetables whole, cutting the larger carrots into thick
slices, trimming the spring onions rather short, and cutting the
tomatoes into wedges. Melt the fat in a heavy-based saucepan.
Add the vegetables at intervals, starting with those which take the
longest time to cook. Put the lid on the pan after each addition and
toss the vegetables in the fat. (Do not add the tomatoes until 5
minutes before serving.) Add the boiling water and salt; use very
little water with the beans and new carrots, etc. Simmer gently
until the vegetables are tender. Season with pepper and serve hot,
garnished with the parsley.

NUT MINCE

6 helpings

200g/7oz shelled nuts
1 medium-sized onion
25g/1oz margarine
150g/5oz dried breadcrumbs
1 × 15ml spoon/1 tablespoon
   mushroom ketchup *or* any
   similar sauce

375ml/¾ pint (approx) vegetable
   stock
salt and pepper

Pass the nuts through a nut mill, process them in an electric blender, or chop very finely. Skin and grate the onion. Melt the margarine in a frying pan and fry the nuts, onion, and breadcrumbs until pale golden. Stir in the ketchup and stock, adding a little extra stock if the mixture is too dry. Season to taste and simmer gently for 20–30 minutes. Serve hot.

THE WALNUT.